Copyright © 2023 by Journey Together LTD

All rights reserved.

No portion of this book may be reproduced in any form without written permission from the publisher or author, except as permitted by U.S. copyright law.

Each day I write, a canvas unfurls,

Ink and ideas, my precious pearls.

A joy to capture thoughts in flight,

Bringing meaning to each day and night.

Words are my colors, sentences my brush,

In this daily practice, I find my hush.

Through tales and poems, I explore the deep,

Finding purpose and solace in every sweep.

In writing, I discover life's grand scheme,

A journey of wonder, like a flowing stream.

With every word, I come alive anew,

For in writing, I find meaning, pure and true.

JOURNEY TOGETHER PUBLISHING

1

Setting, Adventure Prompt:
Describe three distinct locations inside a city:
Saxophones wailing in a darkly lighted, subterranean jazz club where a smokey atmosphere surrounds the patrons.
A hive of sellers selling souvenirs and unique street cuisine in a neon lit night market.
An abandoned warehouse covered with graffiti and featuring vibrant paintings on its walls.

***

2

Continue the narrative: Two characters rush between these locations in an attempt to make a deadline, and we follow them.
The protagonist is a gifted journalist who comes across information that may reveal high-level wrongdoing in the community. They had no

idea that influential people had sent enigmatic operatives to suppress the news. The characters must find the proof they need to achieve their deadline while avoiding their pursuers as they go through the city.

3

Gazing down from a spacecraft in orbit around the planet, you are witnessing astronauts performing experiments on the International Space Station. Continue your story.

4

As you approach the end of your life's journey, take some time to reflect on the lessons life has taught you. Craft a story that inspires others and reminds them of what truly matters.

***

5

Voice Prompt: Consider a library or bookshop that has served as a haven for your intellectual endeavors. Introduce someone to the literary haven's importance and riches as a tour guide.
Continue writing: The tour guide digs into the world of books, offering life-changing tales, information learned, and the undying love of literature that grew inside those bookish individuals.

6

Use this word and start exploring ideas, feelings, and memories surrounding it.
BEGINNING
Continue the story: Write a story in any Genre and Voice.

***

7

Romance, Poetry Prompt: How is your love for someone like an old running shoe? A comfy travel partner, shaped by each step we take together and wearing the scars from the miles we've traveled together. Carry on: Without using the word "love," arrange your lines into a love poem that conveys the warmth and abiding connection that comes from the familiarity of the journey.

8

As a fly on the wall, you observe a team of financial analysts working diligently to navigate the stock market during a tumultuous day. Continue the story.

9

Science Fiction Prompt: An inquisitive robotic mouse named Byte and a sentient tree named Sylvan develop an unexpected telepathic bond in a far-off future where technology and nature coexist together. Write a tale that explores the special relationship between these two creatures and how they work together to resolve environmental issues, solve long standing mysteries, and reconcile the organic and synthetic worlds.

***

10

Write about a day in a town where the grass is blue, and the sky is green due to color inversion. Talk about the bizarre beauty and difficulties of living in this chromatic world.

11

Slice of Life, Setting Prompt: While traveling, your avatar stumbles into an odd museum, such as the Museum of Quirky Collectibles or the Museum of Eccentric Art. What is the museum like?
Continue: Augusta is the curator at the Museum of Eccentric Art. She loves avant-garde and unusual art and can find beauty in the most peculiar things.

12

Consider a week full of daring and exciting deeds. Write about the thrill of living life to the fullest and the dangers you would take.

***

13

Use this word and start exploring ideas, feelings, and memories surrounding it.
TABLE
Continue the story: Write a story in any Genre and Voice.

14

Setting, Adventure Prompt: Describe three very distinct locations inside a city:
A luxurious apartment perched on a high-rise with sweeping views of the cityscape.
A maze-like, old library with obscure passageways and dusty books.
A grungy, illicit fight club known for its violent, unlicensed fights and boisterous patrons.

***

15

Carry on with the story: Craft a captivating story as the influencer embarks on their urban exploration, sharing their experiences, emotions, and how the unique locations they visit shape their perception of the city.

Consider how this journey will impact their online presence and how their followers will respond to this exciting adventure.

16

Voice Prompt: Consider a workplace that was essential in your professional growth. Provide insights on the workplace culture and its influence on your career journey in the voice of a tour guide.

Continue writing: The tour guide describes the challenges, victories, and crucial moments that transpired within those office walls, demonstrating your career's progress.

***

17

Character, Plot Prompt: Your character is using a public toilet to wash their hands. They saw feet in the area beneath a closed stall door. Explain the footwear.

Carry on the narrative: The individual weeping in the restroom is heard by your character. The stranger's voice seemed to be filled with frustration and hopelessness. Why does your personality feel compelled to help this struggling athlete?

18

From the top of a mountain crest, you watch a group of search and rescue experts conduct a mission to help hikers lost in the backcountry. Continue the story.

***

19

Character, Plot Prompt: When a historic, run-down building is set for demolition, Jake, a seasoned construction worker with a heart as tough as his battered work boots, faces an enormous task. Jake sees a chance to save the building and its rich history despite the odds and 'developers' resistance, so he organizes the neighborhood to restore it instead. His steel-toed boots become a sign of perseverance as he works nonstop. By working together, they revitalize the ancient and create a strong link between the past and the future.

20

Describe a medication that does away with the need for sleep. Examine the significant shifts in productivity, daily living, and social norms. Now, tell the story where your character tries it and what transpires thereafter.

***

21

Elena is an artist who makes beautiful, symbolic sandals with embroidery. Her little sandal store becomes a landmark in this cosmopolitan community on the verge of a cultural rebirth.
Elena sets out to unearth long-forgotten family secrets after a strange traveler asks for a pair of shoes that reveal their family's past. Write the story about how Elena and her client learn the value of art in maintaining various customs and overcoming generational divides through Elena's elaborate creations.

22

Scene Prompt: You are peering down from a cliff, watching as a group of environmentalists plant trees to restore a deforested area. Write a story about this.

***

23

Use this word and start exploring ideas, feelings, and memories surrounding it.

HUNGER

Continue the story: Write a story in any Genre and Voice.

24

Mystery Prompt: Your character witnesses a school bus with an odd logo pick up a single student at lunch. A teacher hears what your character says and says, "Tell no one!" Your character looks into it. Carry on writing: Tell us about the student who boarded the bus. Grace, the student, is a calm, kind girl with a soft spot for animals. Your character is intrigued by the compassion and secret connection to nature that she possesses through her eyes.

25

Charlotte ventured into a moonlit cave and observed that the walls were adorned with bioluminescent paintings that recounted a mystical story. Continue the story.

***

26

Setting, Prompt: Describe three distinct locations inside a city:
A calm, secret garden with peaceful ponds and blossoming flowers located in the middle of a busy city.
a disorganized, multi-story indoor bazaar where sellers sell anything from exotic creatures to rare antiquities.
An ancient bookstore with a secret speakeasy lighted by candles behind a modest bookcase.

27

Continue the story: Now, imagine a day in the life of a runway model who encounters these three places during her journey through the city. Craft a narrative that delves into her experiences, the striking contrasts between these locations, and how they affect her perspective as a model. Explore the emotions, surprises, and unexpected encounters that arise as she navigates from the peaceful garden to the bustling market and, finally, to the mysterious speakeasy. How do these diverse settings shape her day, and how will they impact her career and personal life?

***

28

Share the transformative journey of rebuilding your life after a house fire with the item you saved as a symbol of resilience and hope.

29

Write about a time when you were asked to give a eulogy at a funeral, and you struggled to find the right words to honor the departed. How did you convey your emotions during the speech?

30

Use this word and start exploring ideas, feelings, and memories surrounding it.
ORANGE
Continue the story: Write a story in any Genre and Voice.

***

31

Write an inspiring story where your greatest joy is transformed into a gorgeous flowering bush and every time you walk past it and smell the amazing aromas, it gives you spring in your step, and you are able to pay it forward.

32

Science Fiction, Humor Prompt: An extra-terrestrial species keeps Humans as pets. Some owners of people "show" their subjects at events similar to dog shows. Narrate the most exciting parts of the tournament in the host's voice.

Carry on: The winner of the "Best of Show" award is Jackson, a human. He won because of his remarkable ability to adapt to various foreign environments and situations. Jackson is highly regarded by the alien community due to his inventiveness and quick thinking.

***

33

Memoir, Point of View Prompt: Look for or recall a picture of a busy, disorganized kitchen at a holiday get-together with relatives. Describe the scene, the smell of home-cooked food, and the happy pandemonium of family and friends being together.

Carry on the narrative: Write from the perspective of the old matriarch of the family, who has been planning these get-togethers for many years and thinks back on the enduring relationships that were fostered in that kitchen.

34

Write a tale about a village where time stands still, and individuals experience reverse aging. Examine the residents' particular difficulties and viewpoints.

***

35

Consider a surreal library where books transform into other books, and characters appear right out of the pages. Tell the story of a librarian's travels attempting to bring order back.

36

Write a dialogue where your character is at a networking event and can't think of what to say to make a memorable impression on a potential business contact.

37

Memoir, Point of View Prompt: Visualize a book-filled study including leather armchairs and a fireplace. Describe the image, the cozy atmosphere, and the sense of intellectual retreat.
Carry on the narrative: Write as if you were the person in the picture, describing your passion for reading and studying and the wisdom you have discovered inside the book pages.

***

38

In your tale, depict the fourth stop on your character's challenge, a dense forest filled with enchanted beings and perplexing riddles.

39

Talk about a point in your life where you said something you've regretted ever since. Examine your inner turmoil, your perspective, and the lessons you might get from that unfortunate comment.

40

Prompt for Poetry: Allow the dreamy melodies of a pan flute to transport you to a bygone era when mysterious beings and venerable spirits live amidst the tall woods.

Carry on the narrative: Write poetry that invokes the forest's charm, its people's knowledge, and the balance between nature and spirit.

***

41

Memoir, Point of View Prompt: Envision a snapshot of a lively, busy street market in a foreign metropolis. Describe the scene, the bright hues of the exotic spices, and the sounds of people chatting away that combine to create a symphony of life.
Carry on the story: Write from the perspective of the street vendor seen in the picture, narrating the individuals that pass by and their experiences running the market stand.

42

Write about your character's recent visit to a museum where he found himself unable to discuss the artwork with his companion. Did he struggle to find words, or was he simply mesmerized?

***

43

Science Fiction Prompt: In a world where footwear has evolved into advanced, intelligent accessories, a pair of highly experimental smart shoes is accidentally activated. These shoes have the capacity to forecast the wearer's next moves and guide them in the direction of success. Write a narrative that focuses on the moral conundrums, unexpected repercussions, and unprecedented power that arise when a person discovers these exceptional shoes and follows their journey.

44

Use this word and start exploring ideas, feelings, and memories surrounding it.
FRIDAY
Continue the story: Write a story in any Genre and Voice.

***

45

Depict a worn-out pair of hiking boots. Talk about the experiences they've had and the routes they hope to revisit.

46

Conversation Prompt: An elderly woman who is lonely engages a telemarketer in conversation. The telemarketer makes an ineffective attempt to follow their script. Write the conversation.
Continue: The telemarketer divulges information about a secret they have never shared. The telemarketer admits that they hate their work and have always wanted to travel the world and explore other countries among the old woman's stories of loneliness. They talk about the places on their bucket lists and how much they want to live somewhere other than cold calls and sales objectives.

47

Use this word and start exploring ideas, feelings, and memories surrounding it.
GLITTER
Continue the story: Write a story in any Genre and Voice.

***

48

Dialogue Prompt: Character A, a single parent who is having financial difficulties, approaches Character B, their estranged affluent relative, for financial support so they may provide their child with a better life. Character B has shown no support and has remained aloof
Carry on: Character A shows Character B a sincere letter from the kid at the conclusion of their conversation, in which the youngster expresses their desire for a relationship with their relative.

49

You are sitting in a job interview and it was going so well until you were asked an unexpected question, and you struggled to come up with a response. Now, as you are driving home, you are busy formulating the most perfect response.

50

Showcase an abandoned stuffed animal in the attic. Explain the bear's feelings, memories, and desire to be with its owner again.

***

51

Memoir, Point of View Prompt: Looking through your old holiday photos, you 6nd a picture of a sun drenched, weathered beach home. Describe the image, bringing to mind the nostalgic feeling it generates, the sound of the waves crashing, and the scent of salt in the air. Carry on: Write from your parent's perspective, expressing their feelings and observations as they watched you grow up by the sea, and capturing that treasured family occasion at the beach home.

52

Consider the day your dependable old bicycle developed a voice and a personality. Write about the amusing tales it tells and the lessons it has learned from its various travels.

***

53

Character Scene Prompt: Two business partners in a successful startup who have different ideas about where they want to see the firm go. Their divergent approaches and common goals pose a danger to the company's collapse.

Carry on: As they attempt to reconcile their relationship with their professional goals, write the tense exchange that takes place in the boardroom.

54

Use this word and start exploring ideas, feelings, and memories surrounding it.

SPACE

Continue the story: Write a story in any Genre and Voice.

***

55

Romance Prompt: Write the last scene of a relationship that contains a dog, a watch, and a kiss.

Continue Writing: Make a list of story events that may have occurred before this scenario. Alternatively, develop character descriptions for the primary character.

Last Scene: Sarah and Ethan stand on the wooden deck of a quiet cabin by the lake, their devoted labrador, Max, at their side. Ethan gives Sarah an antique wristwatch as a token of their eternal love story. They enjoy a long kiss as the setting sun colors the sky.

56

Describe a recent encounter with an old friend you hadn't seen in years. Did you experience a lull in the conversation, or were you both just momentarily speechless?

Tell about a recent reunion with a long-time friend you hadn't seen in many years. Did you experience a lull in the conversation, or were you both just momentarily speechless?

***

57

Character Prompt: Two childhood buddies who have a hidden attraction for the same person. Their enduring friendship is now challenged by a complicated love triangle.

Carry on: Describe the intensely emotional exchange in which they confess their emotions for the same person, ultimately testing their lifetime relationship.

58

Write a funny tale where your greatest dreaded fear is transformed into a bumbling, lovable sidekick, accidentally saving the day in a series of hilarious mishaps.

59

Write a scene in which, after just a few weeks on a ground-breaking research project, a talented mathematician is dismissed, placing pressure on the colleague who persuaded her to take part.

***

60

Write a romantic poem that explores the idea of love as a cozy, well worn sweater, each thread woven with memories and shared moments. Describe how love provides warmth, coziness, and a sense of belonging even in the coldest times of life, just like a cherished article of clothing. To express the everlasting solace and emotional haven that come from a loving relationship, use rich images and metaphors.

61

Use this word and start exploring ideas, feelings, and memories surrounding it.
SMILE
Continue the story: Write a story in any Genre and Voice.

***

62

Poetry Prompt: Write a moving poem that expresses a handwritten letter's sentimental depth and enduring beauty. Explain the feel of the pen on the paper, how each word is curved precisely, and the close relationship between the sender and the recipient.
Examine how writing can create a connection between people, arouse feelings of nostalgia, and carve love and desire onto the pages, allowing the writer to communicate their most intimate feelings and the reader to relish the priceless sensations that are included.

63

Consider how a single online encounter with a stranger might have changed your life, sparking a lifelong friendship or collaboration.

***

64

Assume that your kitchen blender becomes sentient. Write about the strange discussions it has when blending the fruits and veggies.

65

Adventure Prompt:
While traveling, a character purchases a T-shirt with words in a language they do not understand. Someone reads the shirt and kidnaps them on the first day they wear it. Describe the setting.
Continue: What exactly does the shirt say?

66

Write a scene in which a bright young entrepreneur gets fired from her own firm a week after receiving venture capital investment, forcing the investor who had been a fervent supporter of hers to make a difficult choice...

***

67

Your character reflects on a high school decision, such as choosing a different sports team or club, and explores how it might have impacted their friendships and their social circle.

68

Speak out for your preferred pen. Write about the stories it would tell, ranging from shopping lists to poetry, and the dreams it would assist in putting on paper.

69

Memoir Prompt: Write about a thing you own that is meaningful to you.
Continue: Write about someone who was involved with the thing before you bought it: the previous owner, the maker, the shop owner, and so on.

***

70

Use this word and start exploring ideas, feelings, and memories surrounding it.
PENSIVE
Continue the story: Write a story in any Genre and Voice.

71

Dialogue Prompt: Write a scene where the character says one thing but feels very otherwise. Make subtle references to the character's inner emotions via your speech, gestures, and facial expressions.
Scene Description: Jason is having a talk with his longtime friend Maria in a charming cafe. Maria is eagerly telling him about her approaching wedding. Jason beams and nods, congratulating her, but his sidelong glance and twitchy fingers reveal his secret desire for Maria.

***

72

Continue the story: The tension between Jason and Maria develops as she perceives his disengagement and urges him to express his genuine emotions.

What kind of reaction will Jason have to the emotional exchange?

73

Character A, a skilled writer with a unique book, frantically seeks the approval of Character B, a famously demanding literary agent who has rejected their past work.

Continue the story: Character B ultimately decides to represent Character A at the end of their conversation when they reveal the profoundly emotional inspiration for their novel, building a bond that transcends their professional relationship.

74

Consider a scenario in which you took a chance or spoke up for something in university, and the outcome was something you hadn't anticipated, either positively or negatively.

***

75

Write about the time you lost contact with a buddy you'd known for a long time and the touching reunion you experienced after being apart for years.

76

Fantasy Prompt: A weary vampire, tired of immortality, stumbles upon a magical rite that promises to restore humanity and mortality. However, accomplishing this change comes at the expense of confronting their evil past crimes and defeating an angry coven of other vampires.

77

Dialogue Prompt: Character A, a skilled but suffering chef, requests a good review from Character B, a renowned food critic, in order to preserve their failing business. Character B has continually been critical.
Continue writing: Character B ultimately agrees at the end of their conversation after Character A delivers a magnificent, unforgettable feast that transforms the critic's opinion of their culinary talent.

***

78

A group of explorers discovers a hidden doorway to a parallel universe in a mythical woodland. They must decide whether to join this new realm or return to their own, knowing that the gateway may never be found again.

79

Fantasy Prompt: In a cyberpunk dystopia where memories may be hacked and altered, a rogue hacker discovers a hidden digital world where humanity's collective memory lives. They must confront their own history and alter the future within this virtual environment.

80

Write about a talent or pastime you once briefly explored but eventually gave up on, and consider how it may have been a lifelong interest or vocation.

***

81

Use this word and start exploring ideas, feelings, and memories surrounding it.
STARK
Continue the story: Write a story in any Genre and Voice.

82

Setting, Prompt: Describe three distinct locations:
A luxurious, private art gallery featuring cutting-edge works of art.
An abandoned amusement park with rusting rides and a creepy ambiance that is aged and creaky.
A bright, subterranean club with neon lights and techno music throbbing.

***

83

Continue the story: Envision a day in the life of a successful businessman who finds himself in these contrasting places within a city. Craft a narrative that explores his experiences, emotions, and encounters as he transitions from the world of high-end art to the eerie nostalgia of the abandoned amusement park and, finally, to the pulsating energy of the underground club. How do these diverse settings influence his perspective on business, life, and the city itself? What unexpected revelations or challenges will he face throughout his day?

84

Fantasy Prompt: In a medieval nation controlled by harsh aristocrats, a band of rebels plots to capture a fabled artifact that has the potential to tip the scales. As they progress through their assignment, they discover terrible secrets about their own pasts as well as the actual nature of the artifact.

85

Describe a story set in medieval England, where a key becomes the focus of a local legend, drawing travelers from far and wide to uncover its mysteries.

***

86

Steve opens an ancient, dusty book in the library's collection and finds that the ink on its pages shifted and transformed into an illuminated, animated story.

87

Fantasy Prompt: A little child uncovers an antique, dusty tome buried in his family's home's basement. When he reads the book, he is taken to a magical realm, where he meets a talking animal friend.

88

Write a story about being lost in a foreign place and how the experience led to new friendships and cultural insights.

***

89

Character A, a great scientist, frantically seeks Character B's permission for a controversial research project that may revolutionize their area but has been met with suspicion.

Character B is a well-regarded senior scientist.

Continue reading: Character B ultimately agrees at the conclusion of their conversation when Character A reveals persuasive early data that contradicts the scientific community's views.

90

Create a humorous WANTED ad for a charming cat burglar with a penchant for snatching cozy blankets and building secret blanket forts.

91

A grizzled survivor stumbles into a hidden subterranean community where technology survives in the depths of a post-apocalyptic world.

To safeguard the fragile balance of their own culture, the survivors must decide whether to welcome this evolved world or keep it hidden.

***

92

Write a story that takes place in 1932 Argentina and centers around a teacup that is the key to a family coming to terms with their history and revealing long-kept truths.

93

Fantasy Prompt: A jaded investigator in a noir-inspired metropolis discovers a secret entrance in an abandoned building's basement. As he ventures through it, he discovers a fantasy universe full of mythological animals and a murder mystery that transcends time and reality.

94

Fantasy Prompt: A talented sorcerer discovers an old, enchanted mirror that shows a glimpse of the future. When he looks into it, he sees a cataclysmic occurrence that has the potential to change the path of history. Now, he must figure out how to keep it from occurring again.

***

95

Use this word and start exploring ideas, feelings, and memories surrounding it.
TRANQUIL
Continue the story: Write a story in any Genre and Voice.

96

Write about the day you misplaced a family photo and the touching attempts made by complete strangers to retrieve it.

97

Describe a character named Isabella in the third person, emphasizing how her physical disabilities, personality traits, and relationships have shaped her life in the narrative.

***

98

Science Fiction Prompt: A set of triplets with remarkable abilities is born in a future civilization where genetic modification has become the norm.

However, their gifts come at a price: the more powerful one sibling becomes, the weaker the others become. Describe the complicated relationships and decisions these triplets have to make as they make their way through a society that both admires and fears their amazing abilities. In the end, how will they decide the fate of their planet, maintain equilibrium, and defend one another?

99

Use this word and start exploring ideas, feelings, and memories surrounding it.

RIGHT/WRONG

Continue the story: Write a story in any Genre and Voice.

***

100

Plot Prompt: Name a memorable musical line that you love. Make it the story's title. jot down tale ideas.
Carry on: Use a draft of the tale in which the song's lyrics are used as the opening, closing, or a conversation line.
Title of Song Lyric: "Landslide"
Idea for Story: Sarah is a middle-aged lady who is at a crossroads in her life. She goes back to the rural house where she grew up to face her history, which includes a tense relationship with her mother and a long-lost love.

101

Continue the story: Sarah considers her path and the decisions that led her to this point as she travels back to the locations and experiences of her childhood. The lyrics of the song serve as a moving reminder of the development and changes she has gone through.

***

102

Dialogue Prompt: A Character is a failing artist, and anxious for praise and support &om Character B, is a well-known art critic who has brutally criticized their work.
Continue writing: Character B ultimately decides to mentor Character A at the end of their conversation after witnessing the artist's unwavering dedication and commitment to grow their craft.

103

A brilliant investigator implores a reluctant witness to a crime to testify in court against a dangerous criminal. The witness has been terrified and has refused to comply.
Continue: The Witness ultimately accepts at the end of their conversation when the investigator discloses previously unknown proof that assures their protection throughout the trial.

104

Write a third-person account of a person named Ava, focusing on how her personality qualities and life experiences contribute to internal and external problems in the story.

***

105

Tell a story of how you misplaced a vital document right before an important deadline and how you had to come up with some inventive solutions to get things back on track.

106

Use this word and start exploring ideas, feelings, and memories surrounding it.
VIBRANT
Continue the story: Write a story in any Genre and Voice.

107

Point of View Prompt: Choose a financial scandal news story. Consider yourself an employee of the involved firm, writing from your point of view as you deal with the aftermath, corporate inquiries, and public attention.
Continue reading: Change perspectives to that of an investigative journalist seeking to unearth the truth behind the crisis and bring those involved accountable, illustrating the difficulties of investigative reporting in a complicated corporate context.

***

108

Write a story about discovering an old photo in an attic that sets off a quest to identify the persons it features.

109

Fantasy Prompt: A disillusioned scientist invents a technology that allows folks to explore their dreams amid the neon-lit streets of a futuristic metropolis. As they test the machine, the scientists and their team discover that the dream world is shared by all users, and they discover a secret dimension where nightmares become horrible realities.

Continue writing: The scientists and their crew must navigate the perilous dream realm, confronting their greatest fears and darkest desires, all while an evil creature attempts to swallow their minds.

110

Write a scene set in the grand ballroom of the Roosevelt Hotel, New Orleans, where mischievous twins become unexpected guests at a glamorous event.

***

111

Write a memoir that immerses readers in the atmosphere of a concert hall or music venue that has special significance in your life. Describe the electrifying atmosphere, the reverberations of concerts you will never forget, and the performances that changed your life and will never fade from your memory. In this special location, take your readers on a nostalgic trip through the transforming impact of music and consider how it affected your identity and viewpoint.

112

Write a memoir that transports the reader to a location you once called home, whether it was a modest first apartment or a small college dorm room, during a formative period of your life. Describe the sights, sounds, and smells that defined that space, from the wellworn furniture to the posters on the walls. Explore the recollections and events that unfolded behind those walls, the smiles and the sobs, the connections made, and the lessons discovered. Consider how that location influenced your development, independence, and current self.

***

113

Point of View Prompt: As someone who works closely with one of the politicians who is facing challenges, your character senses the increasing pressure every passing day. The primary responsibility is to control the damage caused by the scandal, but they are constantly reminded that the truth lies beneath layers of deception.
Continue the story: Meanwhile, Sarah, an investigative journalist who is determined to uncover the facts, has heard about the scandal and is relentlessly pursuing it.

114

Iynour story, follows a person who embarks on a journey to understand the meaning behind their repeating dream, uncovering concealed truths, and confronting long-buried memories.

***

115

Character Scene Prompt: A married couple of twenty years are enjoying a dessert that has been a constant in their journey together in a candlelit corner of a fine restaurant. As they look at each other over the last taste of this delicious dessert, a wave of memories and emotions passes over them. Write a moment where the one priceless bite of dessert contains all of the unsaid memories, laughter, and profound love that have defined their marriage.

116

Character Scene Prompt: Two friends, Sarah and Alex, are in a dark art studio surrounded by their colorful canvases. They are each engrossed in their own creative pursuits. However, tension arises as the deadline for a prized scholarship to a famous art school approaches, and their unwavering friendship collides with their individual aspirations. Write a scenario that conveys this.

117

Create a scene where a guesthouse guest, having had a memorable encounter with a mouse, decides to pen a bestselling novel inspired by their experience.

***

118

Fantasy Prompt: Once lauded as a hero, a disgraced knight is condemned to live as a shape-shifting beast. It goes off on a mission to cure the curse, but the voyage takes a dark turn when it comes upon a hidden society of afflicted people who use their infirmities for evil reasons.

Continue writing: To learn the society's actual objective, the disgraced knight must negotiate a labyrinth of intrigue, betrayal, and forbidden magic. Along the journey, they must confront their own inner beast as well as the moral complexity of their task.

119

Tell a story about how you found a restaurant that is a hidden gem with amazing flavors and anecdotes in a remote part of the city.

120

Use this word and start exploring ideas, feelings, and memories surrounding it.

PRISTINE

Continue the story: Write a story in any Genre and Voice.

***

121

Character Scene Prompt: Two siblings meet in their childhood home after years of separation.

Sarah has been taking care of their elderly parents while David returns with a mix of emotions and a sense of responsibility. Their complicated relationship and unresolved family conflicts come to the surface as they work through issues of reconciliation, caregiving, and buried secrets.

122

Write about the time you discovered a family recipe hidden away in a cookbook, and it brought back fond memories and traditions.

123

Point of View and Setting: Describe a frightening, deserted home through the eyes of a paranormal investigator who believes it is haunted.

Continue writing: Describe the same home as a historian who is enthralled by its rich history and hidden mysteries.

***

124

Write an incident about a cockroach that, in a terrifying emergency at a well-known hotel, unexpectedly saves the day.

125

Character Scene Prompt: Two skilled spies, Dmitri and Sarah, who were formerly rivals with a background in espionage and intrigue, find themselves on the same secret assignment among the busy streets of a foreign city. Finding a crucial piece of intelligence is the goal at hand, but a web of complexity and ambiguities is created by their mutual regard and shared background. When Sarah and Dmitri are navigating the high stakes world of espionage once more, create a scenario that explores the complex relationships of trust and suspicion.

***

126

Fantasy Prompt: A couple of professional assassins are hired in a war-torn nation to assassinate a tyrant lord. They find a hidden room housing a sentient, ancient weapon capable of both devastation and salvation as they penetrate the palace.

Continue: The assassins must decide whether to use the weapon to end the dictatorship or to keep it out of the hands of the wrong people. Their decision will determine the fate of the kingdom as well as their own.

127

Science Fiction, Dialogue Prompt: You are a hacker leading a rebellion against the machines in a dystopian civilization ruled by an authoritarian AI. During a daring assault on an AI facility, you come across an artificial organism who has the same voice and demeanor as you. Continue writing: You are able to disable and capture the AI doppelganger. You must now engage in a difficult conversation to discover the origin and purpose of this strangely familiar AI.

***

128

As Henry explored a centuries-old ruin, he discovered a secret chamber filled with enigmatic, glowing crystals that hummed with a strange energy.

129

Tell the tale of how you came into an unknown writer's fascinating life narrative while perusing a handwritten notebook in a secondhand bookstore.

130

Use this word and start exploring ideas, feelings, and memories surrounding it.
ETHEREAL
Continue the story: Write a story in any Genre and Voice.

131

Tell the story of a character who, after a time of emotional distance and cynicism, rediscovers their enthusiasm for love and connection

***

132

Dialogue Prompt: Science Fiction You're an astronaut on a mission to a faraway exoplanet. You come across an extra-terrestrial lifeform that appears to share your thoughts and feelings while exploring the planet's surface.
Continue reading: You make a telepathic link with the alien lifeform and engage in a deep conversation with it, trying to comprehend its nature and the possible insights it has about the cosmos.

133

Point of View Prompt: Your character is a young scientist in the lab, surrounded by colleagues, basking in the glow of a ground-breaking discovery. The excitement is palpable as they recount the long hours of research, tireless experimentation, and the moment when everything finally fell into place.
Continue the story: Dr. Emily Thornton, a skeptic, grapples with the implications of a scientific breakthrough. She scrutinizes the findings despite earlier doubts and confronts the paradigm-shifting consequences of the work.

***

134

Science Fiction, Dialogue Prompt: You come across a fascinating being who shares similar experiences to you but in a post-apocalyptic world devastated by an unknown worldwide calamity. It looks to be the only other person who has survived.
Continue the story: You engage in a meaningful conversation with this intriguing fellow survivor, hoping to uncover the truths of the disaster and why this creature shares your recollections.

135

Write a story on how you overcame adversity to uncover a long forgotten gift or passion in yourself

***

136

Point of View Prompt: As a worker providing humanitarian aid, you see the extent of the natural disaster as you get off the plane and onto the destroyed terrain. The air is thick with grief, and the wreckage is overpowering. You start organizing relief activities and feel a strong feeling of responsibility and purpose amidst the devastation.
Continue: See the disaster from Maria's perspective, a survivor with an unbroken spirit and a resolute will to rebuild. Follow her as she forms relationships with other survivors and celebrates little.

137

Dialogue Prompt: Character A, an environmental activist, implores Character B, a strong business executive, to support a sustainable program. Because of economic constraints, Character B has been dismissed.
Continue: Character B eventually accepts at the end of their conversation when Character A delivers a compelling business case highlighting the long-term advantages of the sustainable project for the company's bottom line.

***

138

Write a story where a character considers how their views about love have changed over time as a result of societal and cultural changes over time

139

Tell about an unexpected gem you discovered while perusing an antique store and its intriguing past.

140

Point of View, Setting Prompt: Describe a grim, post-apocalyptic metropolis through the perspective of a scavenger looking for resources. Continue writing: Describe the same cityscape from the perspective of a group of survivors who have built a close-knit society among the wreckage.

***

141

Detail your morning ritual using a quirky and offbeat vocabulary, from 'tangoing with the razor' to 'moonwalking in boots.

142

In your narrative, offer readers a snapshot of your larger family by giving a single word to each member, showing the intricate mix of personalities that defines your clan.

143

Voice Prompt: Consider your childhood home, the spot where you built numerous memories. Introduce someone to this treasured childhood house in the voice of a tour guide.
Continue: From treehouse expeditions to hidden hideaways and family reunions, narrate significant moments from your upbringing.

***

144

Point of View, Setting Prompt: Describe a crime scene in a poorly lit alley through the eyes of a detective investigating a murder. Continue: Describe the identical criminal scenario through the eyes of a street artist who, owing to their presence at the site, has a unique perspective on the situation.

145

Tell a tale where a character's self-discovery and personal development are sparked by a sneeze.

146

Write about a character who reflects on how their connections with others and their general level of happiness are affected by their self love.

***

147

Use this word and start exploring ideas, feelings, and memories surrounding it.

WHIMSICAL

Continue the story: Write a story in any Genre and Voice.

148

Memoir Prompt: Write a memoir that transports readers to the thrilling world of marathon racing and transforms them. Talk about your own experience, going into detail about the difficult training you endured for months, the highs and lows on race day, and the sheer willpower that got you through those kilometers. Savor the feelings, the companionship of other runners, and the inner strength you find by challenging your body to the maximum. Write about the deep sense of achievement, resiliency, and self-discovery that results from the arduous but worthwhile process of completing a marathon.

***

149

Point of View Prompt: As the controversial art exhibit's artist, your character stands amidst her creations, eager to clarify the deeper meaning behind each piece, brushstroke, and choice of medium. She delves into the emotions, experiences, and societal issues that inspired this artistic journey.

Continue: Let's hear from art critic Alex, who offers a thoughtful critique of her work. Alex analyzes the impact of her creations on the art world and society at large, discussing the controversy, artistic merit, and broader conversation sparked by my provocative pieces.

150

Describe a wonderful trip or vacation spot that has made an indelible effect on you. Introduce a fellow tourist to this magnificent location in the voice of a seasoned traveler.

Continue reading: Write your parents an email describing the life changing experiences and chance meetings that made that journey remarkable, as well as how they affected your viewpoint.

***

151

Explain the emotional path of a podcast presenter with a personal crisis that compels them to face their weaknesses and openly communicate with their listeners about their troubles.

152

Dialogue Prompt: Create a vivid scene that takes place in the bustling courtyard of a university. In this scene, three friends - Alex, Maya, and Sam - share a moment of camaraderie. As the sun shines brightly overhead, the trio engages in a lively discussion about their aspirations, academic goals, and the challenges of university life. Through their dialogue, the distinct personalities, ambitions, and the unbreakable bond that has formed between them during their time at the university should be revealed.

153

Write a story about a time you used the cruelest remark you've ever heard to empower and strengthen yourself and use it as fuel for personal development.

***

154

Point of View: Craft a scene in an opulent casino where a high-stakes poker game is in full swing. Explore the nuances of the game, the psychological warfare, and the thrill of the risk, capturing the gambler's every move and thought.

Then, shift to the viewpoint of a waitress navigating the same casino floor, describing the elegant chaos, the subtle glances exchanged among players, and the mix of excitement and desperation in the air as she serves drinks and observes the drama from the periphery, an unseen observer amidst the glamorous facade.

155

Reflect on the musical journey of your life, choosing a pop song for each decade that represents the background music of your personal growth and evolution.

***

156

Point of View Prompt: Start by examining things from the viewpoint of the brave whistleblower who exposed unethical behavior at work. Describe the internal conflict, moral quandaries, and fear of retaliation they have as they acquire information and, motivated by a feeling of justice, resolve to expose the injustice.

Next, adopt the perspective of a devoted worker who has been blissfully ignorant of the wrongdoing. Describe their amazement, horror, and internal turmoil upon learning of the accusations made against their organization.

157

Point of View Prompt: Choose a news story about a high-profile sporting event. Assume you are a top athlete participating in the championship game, and you are writing from your point of view as you experience the thrill and pressure of the occasion.

Continue: Change your perspective to that of a devoted fan who has been following your profession for years and is emotionally engaged in your success, offering their thoughts on the game's highs and lows.

***

158

Adventure Prompt: Follow your adventurers on an exciting journey across America's diverse landscapes. They trade the mundane for the extraordinary, exploring breathtaking cliffs, busy cities, peaceful plains, and enchanting forests. Their reliable van serves as both a means of transportation and a home on the road. They encounter peculiar roadside attractions, make unusual friendships, and grapple with the challenges of solo travel. Let their van-life odyssey be a testament to the freedom, resilience, and unending spirit of exploration that defines the adventure.

159

Write a tale in which a talk show presenter is stalked mercilessly, and that leads to an engrossing game of cat and mouse that has the potential to change the protagonist's life.

***

160

Use this word and start exploring ideas, feelings, and memories surrounding it.
MAJESTIC
Continue the story: Write a story in any Genre and Voice.

161

Adventure Prompt: Experience a life-changing journey as your main character leaves the bustle of everyday existence to join a remote yoga retreat tucked away in the tranquil heart of the forest. This retreat, which has snow-capped mountains, serene lakes, and lush woods as its background, offers physical rejuvenation, spiritual enlightenment, and connections with a broad community of like-minded individuals.

***

162

Poetry Prompt: Compose a poem that breathes life into seashells, exploring the stories they hold within their delicate curves and intricate patterns. Dive into the imagery of the shore, where each shell carries whispers of the ocean's secrets and the memories of distant tides. Invite the reader to embark on a lyrical journey as seashells become vessels of the time, echoes of the sea's timeless song, and windows to the mysteries of the deep.

163

DIY home renovation project. Write your dialogues between the partners as they try and work together on the project, the pitfalls of inexperience, budget overruns, and structural mishaps.

164

Tell the story of an occasion when you received the greatest compliment you have ever received in the form of an anonymous message that made you want to 6nd out who sent it.

***

165

Memoir Prompt: Write a captivating memoir that transports readers to the world of a stable. Share your personal encounters and cherished memories with horses. Describe the daily routine, the relationship with these majestic creatures, and the lessons learned. Celebrate the enduring appeal of these four-legged friends and their life-changing impact on you.

166

Character Prompt: Meet Max, the quirky brewmaster behind "Max's Brew Haven," a microbrewery famous for its unique and experimental brews. Max's unusual brewing techniques and contagious enthusiasm attract newcomers and devoted patrons to his microbrewery, where each beer has a funny story. Discover how Max's personality shapes the microbrewery's identity and enhances the brewing experience for visitors.

167

Write a little narrative that revolves around a character's search in a busy farmers' market for the ideal cucumber.

***

168

Poetry Prompt: Write a poem that embodies the tenacity and grace of a willow tree softly swaying in the wind. To portray the tree's long, elegant branches-which like flowing drapes that brush the earth-use vibrant images. Examine the feelings and tales that could be hidden behind its cover, the secrets it has seen, and the comfort it provides to those who seek cover under its weeping branches. Celebrate the willow's capacity to flex but never break

169

Use this word and start exploring ideas, feelings, and memories surrounding it.
ARROW
Continue the story: Write a story in any Genre and Voice.

170

As an events coordinator, compose a guide to planning a wedding, detailing everything from vendors to weather and family drama. And what do you do when there is a Bridezilla on the loose?

***

171

Romantic Comedy Prompt: Craft a delightfully quirky romance scene set in a picturesque park. Picture a couple who have planned the perfect picnic on a sunny day, complete with a checkered blanket and a basket of delicious treats. But there's one problem: a mischievous group of squirrels has taken a keen interest in their picnic, staging a hilarious raid on their sandwiches and snacks. Explore how this whimsical encounter sets the stage for a unique and memorable romance, where love blooms amidst the antics of the park's most notorious picnic bandits.

172

Mystery prompt: The proprietor of an antique shop finds a worn-out diary with enigmatic notes and illustrations that allude to an unresolved historical mystery. Discover a lost history chapter and go back in time with a committed historian as they solve the journal's mysterious riddles.

***

173

Point of View Prompt: Select a story on a game-changing technological advance. Assume you're a tech entrepreneur who had a key part in developing the technology, and you're writing from your point of view as you consider the possibilities.
Continue writing: Change your perspective to that of an ethical hacker who sees the new technology as a possible danger to privacy and security and is committed to disclosing its flaws.

174

Create a scene where a chef at a posh restaurant tries out novel foods based on kiwis, pushing the frontiers of cuisine and shocking patrons.

175

It's been one of those days; everything that can go wrong does. This evening, you go on a blind date, but this, too, is full of disaster, with ingredients like awkward silences, miscommunications, and unfortunate wardrobe malfunctions.

***

176

Explain a character's endeavor to replicate their grandmother's renowned preserves, emphasizing the sentimental bond with family customs.

177

Use this word and start exploring ideas, feelings, and memories surrounding it.
CHAOS
Continue the story: Write a story in any Genre and Voice.

178

Use this word and start exploring ideas, feelings, and memories surrounding it.
RECIPES
Continue the story: Write a story in any Genre and Voice.

***

179

Imagine a dozen fairies dancing gracefully among a field of bluebells, their ethereal performance captivating onlookers. They had no idea the twelfth fairy held the key to a spectacular discovery.

180

Adventure Prompt: Follow a girl and her dog on a thrilling journey from their home to the wild. As they overcome obstacles and discover hidden treasures, their bond grows stronger. Together, they learn about love, devotion, and adventure.

181

Use this word and start exploring ideas, feelings, and memories surrounding it.
WRISTWATCH
Continue the story: Write a story in any Genre and Voice.

***

182

Write a step-by-step manual on organizing a disastrous school field trip, complete with transportation issues, unruly students, and unexpected emergencies.

183

Character Prompt: Meet Sylvia, a precise accountant passionate about numbers. She balances finances and crunches statistics for clients, both big and small. Her well-organized chaos of colorful notes and trusty calculator are her tools. Sylvia solves Financial puzzles and spots irregularities others might miss. She's also an avid mystery reader.

184

Write a funny story about a town's watermelon-themed festival, filled with watermelon-themed activities, competitions, and eccentric characters.

***

185

Share a tale about a humanitarian endeavor your character briefly became fervently involved in but ultimately lost interest in.

186

Romantic Comedy Prompt: A young romance unfolds at a busy skatepark where Jake and Mia cross paths. Jake tries to impress Mia with his skateboarding skills but takes a tumble, making Mia laugh. Sitting on a bench, snacking, and discussing music, they discover a connection through their shared humor. Their unpredictable and delightful romance begins.

187

These two characters don't have a clue about cars. Yet here they are, trying their hand at DIY car repair. It unfolds in chaos, the missteps and mishaps that occur while trying to fix a vehicle without proper knowledge.

***

188

Location, Prompt: Describe three distinct locations
A luxurious apartment on the top level of an opulent hotel with expansive views.
A bustling subway station is said to be haunted in the early hours.
A gentleman's club where the members enjoy special whiskey.

189

Continue the story: Explore the life of a skateboarding champion in this city. Describe their experiences, emotions, and encounters throughout the day as they travel between these various locations. How their opulent apartment reflects their success and lifestyle. Discover the secrets and thrills they encounter while skateboarding in the early morning at the haunted subway station. See how they connect with their Sponsors at the gentleman's club after a day of exhilarating skateboarding. Dive into their unique blend of athleticism, adventure, and style that defines their life in the city.

***

190

Point of View, Setting Prompt: Describe a peaceful, sun-kissed beach at dusk through the perspective of a tired traveler looking for comfort and rest.

Continue writing: Describe the same beach through the perspective of a native who takes solace in the familiarity of the waves and the memories they contain.

191

Use this word and start exploring ideas, feelings, and memories surrounding it.

LUMINOUS

Continue the story: Write a story in any Genre and Voice.

192

Romantic Comedy Prompt: In a bustling marketplace, two characters accidentally bump into each other while reaching for the last slice of pizza. A playful argument ensues, drawing the attention of amused onlookers. They share the slice and sit at a nearby table with a bottle of rose wine. With pizza sauce on their cheeks, they discover an unexpected connection amidst the chaotic marketplace, sparking a heartwarming romance.

***

193

A moment of distraction can result in a missed connection with a soulmate, leaving one to ponder what might have been.

194

Your character explores the consequences of their unrealized literary dreams through a collection of books they have passionately assembled but hardly ever read.

195

Your character is trying his best to arrange a surprise vacation for his parent's anniversary. But disaster is the name of the game, from last-minute changes, travel mishaps, and unexpected destinations that lead to chaos and confusion.

***

196

Craft a tale where a girl's wings become an emblem of intrigue and wonder, compelling her to search for answers and embark on a magical quest.

197

Romantic Comedy Prompt: Jane and Michael's competitive tennis match turns hilariously awkward when Jane accidentally hits an apple pie &om a nearby picnic area. Amidst laughter and apologies, they share a slice of the squashed pie and sparks fly between them, leading to an unexpected romance.

198

Mystery prompt: A well-known psychic foretells a string of mysterious happenings that appear to be happening, which causes a close-knit community to become more terrified and hysterical. Take a journey with a skeptic journalist to solve the riddles surrounding the psychic's predictions and reveal the truth concealed in the coded signals.

***

199

Write a narrative about a futuristic device that claims to be able to understand and translate animal languages but whose complex interface leaves you perplexed by what the animal kingdom has to say.

200

Write a story about a catastrophic holiday dinner detailing culinary disasters, family squabbles, and unexpected dietary restrictions.

201

Romantic Comedy Prompt: Imagine a charmingly awkward moment at the local grocery store. As Sarah, a cashier with a penchant for klutziness, accidentally knocks over a display of milk cartons, her face turns beet red as the contents spill everywhere. Enter James, a helpful customer with a quick wit and a broom in hand, who rushes to her aid. With a playful exchange of banter and shared laughter, James helps Sarah clean up the milky mess. As they bond over the situation's absurdity, their unexpected connection takes root.

***

202

Poetry Prompt: Craft a poetic ode to the symphony of a bustling cityscape. Dive into the bustle of city life, where voices make a chattering chorus, footfall provides a pounding beat, and blaring horns turn into brassy sounds. Discover how the city's soundscape changes as day breaks and twilight approach, from the soft murmur of the morning to the booming din of rush hour to the soft lullaby of night. Your poetry must create a rich soundscape, highlighting the tunes and harmony concealed within the city's daily turmoil.

203

While trekking in the wilderness, Lily stumbled upon a solitary glade where fireflies danced in patterns that seemed to mimic constellations in the night sky.

204

Use this word and start exploring ideas, feelings, and memories surrounding it.
TORN
Continue the story: Write a story in any Genre and Voice.

***

205

It's a 5-year-old girl's birthday party, but oh dear, the treasure hunt is all just going wrong. Tell about this disaster as her older sibling included poorly drawn maps and false clues. The misadventures are just at every turn.

206

Explain a futuristic gadget that you can't understand the cryptic readouts and symbols on, yet it says it can analyze dreams.

207

In an instant, a baby's first smile can ignite boundless joy in the hearts of parents, capturing a treasured moment of unadulterated happiness. Write your story around these feelings.

***

208

Romantic Comedy Prompt: Picture this: a funny mistake happens at a busy flea market. Sarah, an enthusiastic and quirky vendor, is showing off her unique collection of vintage boots. In her eagerness to attract potential buyers, she accidentally grabs two mismatched boots. Enter Sam, a similarly eccentric customer with a taste for peculiar fashion, who buys the odd boots without realizing the mistake. When he returns to Sarah's booth, proud of his "bold fashion choice," they both laugh when they discover the truth. This amusing encounter leads to a special connection that blossoms.

209

Write a memoir that takes readers to Australia's wild, expansive outback in the 1920s. Tell about your experience while evoking a clear image of the untamed terrain, the strong local communities, and the difficulties encountered in this hostile setting.
Think back on the unforgettable moments, interactions with native cultures, and the resilient spirit that shaped your stay in the outback. Through your memoir, offer a glimpse into a bygone era where the frontier spirit of adventure and survival thrived amidst the stunning backdrop of the Australian wilderness.

***

210

Use this word and start exploring ideas, feelings, and memories surrounding it.
BURGUNDY
Continue the story: Write a story in any Genre and Voice.

211

Use this word and start exploring ideas, feelings, and memories surrounding it.
MOVIES
Continue the story: Write a story in any Genre and Voice.

212

Write a story about your character's business venture that is destined for failure, including misguided strategies, unreliable partners, and financial mismanagement.

***

213

Mystery prompt: A tiny village is experiencing a number of weird incidents, including reports of strange lights in the night sky and mysterious patterns carved into agricultural fields. Join a group of scientists, skeptics, and believers as they investigate the inexplicable events in an effort to find solutions.

214

Use this word and start exploring ideas, feelings, and memories surrounding it.
WISTFUL
Continue the story: Write a story in any Genre and Voice.

215

Describe a home robot that possesses sophisticated learning skills, but you have no idea how to program it to accomplish simple chores.

***

216

Mystery prompt: A lighthouse keeper in a quaint seaside hamlet vanishes without a trace, leaving behind a logbook full of mysterious entries. To locate the missing keeper, a detective, and a marine biologist must unravel the secrets of the lighthouse as they explore the wonders of the water.

217

Write a story where a buddy phones to ask about a viral video that appears to show you dancing in a packed city plaza with a flash mob. What gave rise to this spontaneous dance?

218

Point of View Prompt: Choose a story about a high-profile courtroom trial. Assume you are a defense attorney representing the accused and writing from your point of view while fighting relentlessly to prove your client's innocence.

Continue writing: Transition to the perspective of a jury who is wrestling with the weight of the evidence and the duty of deciding the destiny of the accused.

***

219

Character Scene Prompt: Two long-time neighbors who are both interested in acquiring the same lovely house that has recently come on the market. Their rivalries threaten to overwhelm their relationship. Continue writing: Capture their rising competition as they both try to outmaneuver the other in their effort to obtain the property, putting their relationship at peril.

220

Mystery prompt: After receiving the inheritance of a lonely mountain lodge, a family finds a hidden chamber with cryptic writings and enigmatic items. Discover the mysteries surrounding the former owner of the lodge, a talented but secretive inventor, by accompanying them on a spooky voyage of discovery.

221

A lightning storm destroys a childhood treehouse. Explain that eerie feeling as the night sky darkens before lightning strikes.

***

222

Prompt Poetry: Craft a poem that explores the profound stillness and beauty of a deep winter's morning. Describe the scene where the world is in a silent state of slumber and the air is crisp, covered in a glittering patchwork of snow. Draw a picture of the soft frost on windows, the faint play of sunshine on frozen limbs, and the muffled crunch of snow beneath your feet. Convey the calm and reflective ambiance of this snowy environment, when everything appears to be frozen in time and the beauty of the season is revered.

223

Mystery prompt: A journalist follows a trail of corruption and conspiracy inside a formidable business empire after receiving a series of enigmatic correspondences sent anonymously. Discover the world of high-stakes journalism, corporate espionage, and secret objectives as one message at a time the truth is exposed.

***

224

Character Scene Prompt: A detective and a journalist are both desperate to learn the truth in a high-profile murder case. They have a history of disagreements over tactics and ethics.
Continue: Write a heated discussion between the investigator and the journalist as they strive to outsmart each other while grappling with their opposing ways of solving the case.

225

Craft a story in which your friend calls to discuss what they saw at a science fair. Have a discussion with your equally nerdy friend about what fascinates you about the project or experiment.

226

Use this word and start exploring ideas, feelings, and memories surrounding it.
CAPTIVATED
Continue the story: Write a story in any Genre and Voice.

***

227

Abeloved camping area is destroyed by a forest fire. Write about the strange shift of the smoke-choked sky as flames approach.

228

Mystery prompt: A terrifying mystery is concealed in a centuries-old castle in the isolated Scottish Highlands. On tour, a group of history enthusiasts and paranormal investigators must interpret cryptic clues and deal with unsettling incidents in order to learn about the castle's troubled past.

229

Mystery prompt: In a run-down old bookshop, an old map that is said to point to a mythical city of riches reappears. Discover the adventures of a bold archaeologist and a shrewd treasure seeker as they solve riddles, avoid danger, and search for unfathomable wealth.

***

230

Write a narrative where an aunty calls you to discuss a social media post of you volunteering at a wildlife sanctuary. Share the experiences and what has led to your involvement.

231

Mystery prompt: A reclusive writer passes away inexplicably, leaving behind a number of incomplete manuscripts that could hold the key to a secret literary masterpiece. Explore the mysterious world of books and perplexing hints while a committed admirer endeavors to finish the author's last work.

232

Mystery prompt: A famous art collector's home is broken into, and one of the gallery's well-guarded masterpieces is removed. Put yourself in the shoes of the astute but reclusive investigator who has to work his way through a maze of lies, counterfeits, and rivalries within the art world to retrieve the stolen masterpiece.

***

233

Craft a narrative about Thanksgiving where a well-intentioned attempt at a healthier version of a classic dish ended in culinary disappointment.

234

Poetry Prompt: Write a poem that conveys the peaceful wonder of dawn on a farm in Africa. Describe the soft, gentle warmth that awakens the earth as the first blush of dawn caresses the horizon. Allow the reader to experience the soothing symphony of birdsong, the gentle patter of leaves, and the far-off whisper of farm life awakening. Your poetry should convey the serene beauty of this rural African setting, where the earth rises in time with the cycles of nature, and the day begins with promise.

235

Mystery prompt: The beloved local librarian in a sleepy English community is discovered dead in the book stacks, and the sole clue is a mysterious note discovered inside a book. Discover the truth as the inquisitive members of the book club become amateur detectives to investigate the mysterious murder.

***

236

A beloved park is engulfed by a huge sinkhole. As you tell the story, capture the spooky and unnerving color scheme of the sky before this great calamity.

237

Yesterday, your character attended a masquerade ball where they unexpectedly ran into a long-lost friend. Write about the mysterious events of that day that led you to attend the ball.

238

Share the amusing escapades of your shrunken character as they navigate a kitchen turned into a vast landscape, facing culinary challenges and meeting kitchen utensils.

***

239

Use this word and start exploring ideas, feelings, and memories surrounding it.
APPLES
Continue the story: Write a story in any Genre and Voice.

240

Craft a narrative where a family's ordinary backyard becomes a setting for an extraordinary bond with a friendly alien, forever shifting their perspective on the cosmos.

241

Setting, Adventure Prompt: Describe three distinct locations
A mysterious cave beckons with its moss-covered entrance, leading to a world of shadowy wonder where stalactites hang like ancient chandeliers.
A forest that stands in quiet reverence, where towering trees create a lush canopy, their leaves dappled with sunlight.
Perched on the edge of the crystal-clear lake, the quaint rustic lake house's wooden exterior mirrored in the tranquil waters.

***

242

Continue the story: In this adventure, a group of school kids journeys through three unique locations. They explore a moss-covered cave, a serene forest with hidden clearings and curious wildlife, and a lakeside retreat ideal for swimming, fishing, or relaxation. How do these contrasting settings shape their day of exploration, and what lessons or memories will they take home from their urban adventure?

243

Use this word and start exploring ideas, feelings, and memories surrounding it.
RADIANCE
Continue the story: Write a story in any Genre and Voice.

244

Mystery prompt: During an expedition in the middle of the African jungle, a wellknown archaeologist vanishes. Experience an exhilarating journey as a group of detectives, under the direction of a perceptive wildlife biologist, trace the enigmatic trail the missing scientist left behind, discovering lethal threats and archaic mysteries in the process.

***

245

Share your memories of the local landmarks and shops that defined your upbringing.

246

Your friend calls in a panic, saying they spotted you in the emergency room yesterday. What led to your unexpected hospital visit?

247

Prompt for Memoir: Write about a possession that holds special meaning for you.

Carry on the Story: Write about a person who had any connection to the item before you acquired it, such as the maker, the store owner, or a prior owner.

Object Synopsis: Nathan muses over his father's ancient, leatherbound diary, which is chock full of handwritten notes documenting a lifetime of learning and insight. Nathan finds solace and direction in it.

***

248

Continuing: Nathan discovers the tale of a knowledgeable mentor named Samuel, who was not only his father's close friend but also the one who gave him the diary, as he reads through the book's previous entries. Nathan retains the practice of journaling his own experiences, and he finds great value in Samuel's profound insights and life teachings.

249

Mystery prompt: A famous socialite's precious diamond necklace disappears off her neck at an opulent masquerade event. As they race against time to uncover the crafty thief before the night is up, join the exclusive party guests-each of whom is hiding secrets of their own.

250

Your character has just spent a week-long holiday with their family. It had many emotional highs and lows. Reflect on the lessons learned from this time spent with family.

***

251

Poetry Prompt: Compose a vivid poem that transports the reader to the heart of a tempest's fury, where the wild moorland stands defiant against the untamed power of nature. Describe how the roaring winds, the unrelenting rain, and the churning clouds collide with the rocky landscape, evoking the forces of nature at work. To illustrate the turbulent beauty of this wild display, where the moorland transforms into a battlefield and a monument to nature's unwavering spirit, use powerful metaphors and vivid images.

252

Craft a narrative where your character's mysterious misfortune leads to a day spent exploring the secret world of an abandoned dollhouse in their attic, complete with tiny inhabitants.

253

List the flowers that flourished in the flower beds of your childhood neighborhood.

***

254

Use this word and start exploring ideas, feelings, and memories surrounding it.
BITTERSWEET
Continue the story: Write a story in any Genre and Voice.

255

Dialogue Prompt: Set the scene in the bustling dance studio lobby: a bunch of dancing moms, each with their own distinct flair and stage mom energy, are having a comically competitive conversation about their kids' impending performance. As they negotiate the competitive world of dancing, their discourse should be full of humorous exaggerations and eccentric behaviors, ranging from lavish outfit ideas to outrageous prop recommendations.

***

256

Point of View Prompt:
Describe a courtroom during a high-profile trial through the eyes of a defense counsel battling for their client's innocence.
Continue the story: Describe the same courtroom through the eyes of a jury striving to stay impartial in the middle of the case's media frenzy.

257

Write a story about an old man sitting on his front porch reminiscing about his academic milestones and their lasting impact on his personal and professional life.

258

Craft an intriguing narrative about the origins of a magical, talking animal who became a beloved character in folklore.

***

259

In the narrative, depicts the zany escapades of your pet dragon as it tries to fit in with humans, wreaking comedic chaos along the way.

260

Romance, Poetry Prompt: Write a love poem that is influenced by the classic pearl string, which is a representation of grace and refinement. Imagine a situation where a lover gives this beautiful gift to their sweetheart, each pearl representing a treasured memory they have shared. Urge the poet to examine the pearls' delicate beauty and exquisite textures, as well as how they reflect the individual characteristics of the wearer.

261

Fantasy Prompt: A character is putting together a jigsaw puzzle when they see the image is of their own kitchen - with one exception. Instead of a window, there's a mysterious doorway dripping with unearthly hues.
Continue writing: They glance up from the puzzle, and as they gaze at the enigmatic gateway, they are compelled to enter it. What adventures are in store for them on the other side?

***

262

Write the fable of an extraordinary flower that inspired the creation of Mother's Day.

263

Narrate your story about one of your travel experiences and explore how it has contributed to your sense of adventure and desire to explore new horizons.

264

Scene and Dialogue Prompt: A gifted student in their final year of high school approaches their biology lab partner for a prom date with a sophisticated "promposal." Pen the scenario. What is the lab partner's reaction?

Carry on: At their 20-year reunion, the two reunite. Write the conversation. Memories of the prom come rushing back, along with the turns life has taken them on, as they reunite after twenty years apart. What unexpected shocks are in store for them at this reunion, and how have their lives diverged?

***

265

Mystery Prompt: A fisherman in a little seaside village finds a locked chest hidden in the sand that is said to contain the key to a lost pirate treasure.

Uncover the mystery of the chest's origin and the truth about the illustrious pirate's legacy as history fans and treasure seekers swarm the town.

266

Use this word and start exploring ideas, feelings, and memories surrounding it.

DESOLATE

Continue the story: Write a story in any Genre and Voice.

***

267

Science Fiction Prompt: Unintentionally, a future innovation ends up in the present. How is it used? And what cultural disruption does it cause?
Carry on the Story: The persona who sent the innovation seeks to make things right.
Description of the invention: A futuristic Universal Translator that can translate any language into its original tongue appears in the present. But inadvertently, technology begins interpreting spoken words and ideas, leading to worldwide misunderstandings and confusion.

268

Imagine the legendary backstory of the Tooth Fairy, her first encounter with a youngster's lost tooth, and the custom that she started.

269

Write a story about a character's five most important professional experiences, including the obstacles they overcome and the lessons they discovered along the way.

***

270

Point of View Prompt: Describe a lonely, secluded lodge in the forest from the perspective of a survivalist preparing for a storm. Continue writing: Describe the same cabin through the perspective of a lost hiker who comes across it while looking for refuge from the elements.

271

In your narrative, depict a typical morning where your character has 'mug conversations' with their coffee.

272

Poetry Prompt: Write a fanciful poem that dances in the moonlight, imagining it to be a cunning heavenly feline that prowls the night sky. Discover how the moonlight leaves a trail of mysteries and magic in its wake as it peeks through curtains, dances over roofs, and teases the world below. Let the moonlight cat's silver paws scatter dreams among the stars, and let its midnight adventures enchant your poetry.

***

273

Use this word and start exploring ideas, feelings, and memories surrounding it.
NEIGHBOR
Continue the story: Write a story in any Genre and Voice.

274

Your character is about to make a decision that will change their life. Let's combine a few lies and secrets to reveal the intricate details that shaped their decision.

275

Describe the obstacles and victories of your character as they embrace their miniature form and embark on a quest to help a tiny community of woodland creatures.

***

276

Science Fiction Prompt: In the future, when kids lead the way in research and invention, a group of young pals discovers an enigmatic object in their backyard.
It's a tiny, apparently malfunctioning quantum computer. They unintentionally discover its amazing power as they work to fix and comprehend it, giving them the ability to control reality and time.

277

Recreate the peaceful environment of a zen garden with precisely raked sand and carefully placed stones that encourage contemplation.

278

Point of View Prompt: Choose a protest or social movement. Consider yourself a passionate activist in the center of the movement, writing from your point of view while detailing your reasons and ambitions. Continue writing: Change to the perspective of a law enforcement officer entrusted with preserving order during the demonstration, emphasizing the difficulties and dangers.

***

279

Write about a memorable meeting you had with a popular person or celebrity. To make your story more interesting, include a lie and a secret.

280

Describe the splendor and calm of a moonlit desert landscape, where the sand glows gently under the silvery light.

281

Use this word and start exploring ideas, feelings, and memories surrounding it.
NOSTALGIC
Continue the story: Write a story in any Genre and Voice.

***

282

Write about the shadowy figures on your wall speaking in a language of symbols and metaphors, urging you to interpret their profound messages.

283

Share the calming ambiance of an idyllic lakeshore cabin surrounded by serene waters and the rustling of leaves in the wind.

284

Romantic Poetry Prompt: Write a romantic poem that incorporates a love tale with the mesmerizing sounds of a cello. Imagine a moonlight, romantic moment where a talented cellist serenades their sweetheart. Examine the feelings evoked by the song and the way it floats across the atmosphere, blending with the two lovers' pounding hearts. Urge the poet to celebrate the ability of music to bring people together in a symphony of love by utilizing the sensual tones of the cello to intensify the passion.

***

285

Point of View, Setting Prompt: Describe a gorgeous, extravagant ballroom during a huge masquerade party through the eyes of a socialite in attendance.
Continue: Describe the same ballroom through the eyes of a mystery stranger who infiltrated the celebration with a secret intent.

286

Write a narrative about a noteworthy cultural or artistic event that your character attended. To enhance a sense of mystery, combine a lie and a secret.

287

Dialogue Prompt: Create a setting in which Sarah, Emily, and Lisa, three home schooling mothers, meet for their weekly support coffee in a comfortable living room. They chat about their successes, struggles, and distinctive home-schooling methods while sipping tea and watching their kids play nearby. Examine the group's varied viewpoints and personalities while emphasizing how their camaraderie and common experiences give them priceless support for their academic endeavors.

***

288

Point of View Prompt: Describe a crowded, chaotic hospital emergency room as seen through the eyes of a stressed-out clinician at a key juncture.
Continue writing: Describe the same emergency department from the perspective of a patient's family member who is awaiting word on their loved one's status.

289

A need for anything Mediterranean? Our delicious gyro is a culinary wonder. You'll be taken to the bright beaches of Greece with every mouthful. Opa! Write about an experience.

290

Personal Opinion: Choose a space exploration mission news story. Assume you are an astronaut on a spacecraft, writing from your point of view as you prepare for the voyage into the unknown.
Continue writing: Change to the perspective of a scientist on Earth who is looking forward to the mission's data and discoveries, expressing their hopes and expectations.

***

291

Write a story of a special meal that featured a dish so unappetizing, it became the source of laughter and teasing for years to come.

292

Use this word and start exploring ideas, feelings, and memories surrounding it.

JUBILANT

Continue the story: Write a story in any Genre and Voice.

293

A phone ringing from the cargo hold is heard by the captain when they are flying during a rainy night and experiencing turbulence. For what reason does this cause people to second-guess their choice to be in the air?

***

294

Poetry Prompt: Let your mind be soothed by the gentle, melodious chords of a piano. Imagine yourself alone on a peaceful, moonlight sailboat with only the soft sound of the water lapping against the hull for company.
Carry on the story: Write poetry that conveys the peace of the ocean, the moon's gentle reflection on the water, and the sailor's introspective voyage beneath the stars at night.

295

Delight in the taste of our succulent barbecue ribs, carefully roasted over low heat and covered in our proprietary sauce. Prepare yourself for a taste explosion that will be unlike any other.

***

296

Science Fiction Prompt: One fateful day, a teenager finds that their regular microwave oven has a peculiar side effect that causes it to open a tiny gateway to a different universe each time something heats up inside of it. Write a narrative that examines the unforeseen events, misadventures, and difficulties they encounter as they start using their microwave to communicate with this weird parallel reality. What mysteries, perils, or surprising connections lie beyond?

297

In a touching letter to a withering houseplant, describe the bond that has developed over the years and the desire to see it flourish with renewed vitality.

298

Craft your own story about the lessons and reflections that arise during your Snal week as you look back on your life's journey and what truly matters.

***

299

A climber nearing the top of a treacherous peak hears music reverberating through the mountain pass. Why does this sound make individuals feel anxious and uneasy?

300

Use this word and start exploring ideas, feelings, and memories surrounding it.
SOCKS
Continue the story: Write a story in any Genre and Voice.

***

JOURNEY TOGETHER PUBLISHING

Keep an eye out for additional books in this series.

Scan the QR code to discover more of our exciting products!

www.ingramcontent.com/pod-product-compliance
Lightning Source LLC
Chambersburg PA
CBHW030121100526
44591CB00009B/481